Dyptoe
The Yellow-Eyed Penguin

Mary Taylor

SCHOLASTIC
AUCKLAND SYDNEY NEW YORK LONDON TORONTO

Dyptoe the yellow-eyed penguin dives. His flippers are as wings and he steers with his feet. He flies through the yellow water, the green water, the blue water, diving deep down to the inky-black water.

Dyptoe the lone hunter skims the ocean floor. He strikes at a flash of silver and gulps the whole fish. Another strike, another fish. Then he loops through a dark, rocky arch and surges upwards. He leaves the black water, the blue, the green and breaks through the yellow water into air and takes breath.

He floats on the sea, rests on the waves.

Before Time began, penguins like him have breathed, dived and rested like this, in oceans sleepy or wild with storm. Penguins belong to the sea, just like the fish and dolphins, the sharks and whales, the seahorses, squid, sponges, shells and seaweeds.

Dyptoe, creature of the sea, is well-fed. He dives again just to somersault in the green water, shoot skywards into the air and arc down again — all for the joy of it.

For this is the way of the yellow-eyed penguin, the hoiho.

3

Long Ago

A penguin surfs into shore on the breakers, yellow crown and yellow eye above the foam. Then he's covered again.

There are penguins everywhere. Penguins airborne, leaping the waves, penguins diving through swirling kelp, penguins bounding, flying through the sea and the breakers, penguins sliding belly-on-sand. As the wave glides back they stand erect, and walk on pink webbed feet from the sea, looking up the beach, down the beach, scanning the shore for dangers. Then they run, slap-slap fast, over the shiny sand. Nearby, on the biggest rock, the sea lion raises his head — but today he's too slow.

The penguins gather on the rocks, holding up their flippers to preen underneath, dipping their bills into the oil glands above their tails and smoothing down ruffled feathers. They trumpet and chatter and bow to each other.

A shadow passes over.

They cringe and scatter.

Then they're back on the rocks, for the shadow is only a wind-driven cloud, not the huge-clawed giant eagle which preys on seabirds like penguins.

5

Sleek, well-fed and groomed, the penguins waddle alone or in pairs into the forest that shades the golden sand. There are penguin paths into the forest, over soft moss, filmy ferns and tiny orchids; cool earth paths under purple flowers, shrubs and vines, across tinkling, brown streams; paths which lead deep into the green shade. Here the tree ferns arch overhead, and still higher grow the forest giants: kamahi, rimu, matai, totara.

The forest is rich with berries and flowers, insects, spiders, moths, worms, snails and beetles. Coloured geckos and skinks dart amongst the leaves. The tuatara poses on his boulder, undisturbed by the crashing and thrashing of branches as the huge moa tramples past.

Yellow penguin eyes close to the evensong of the kokako, huia, saddleback, tui and bellbird. Then the songbirds grow quiet, and shuffle their wings.

Black night comes with the screech of the bright-eyed morepork, the chuckle of the laughing owl, and bat shapes loosening from trees. The kiwi snuffles amongst the leaves on the forest floor and the kakapo browses the mosses.

Safe and cool, the penguins rest in their chosen places of dark shadow beside massive fallen logs and rocks. Each pair settles for the night. They can hear other penguins but they can't see them. This is where they lay their eggs and raise their young, here under the protection of the forest.

This is the way of the yellow-eyed penguin.

7

Today

Hoiho have walked this land for many millions of years. Dyptoe lives today but he sees the world exactly as his ancestors did. He's a bird of the ocean by day and a bird of the forest by night.

Today's world holds dangers worse than sea lions or eagles.

On the Otago Coast the land is still here but the forest is gone. Now there are fences and grass, sheep and cattle. The few remaining penguins return to the land of their ancestors to do what penguins have always done.

At sea, the winter wind screams in icy fury and the waves break into a thousand white horses. All day Dyptoe the yellow-eyed penguin has hunted. As the clouds darken, he turns for the shore. He must find his mate, Marina, and rest until dawn.

He circles in the breakers, searching the beach with his yellow eyes. In the shallow water he stands and then runs slap-slap fast over the wet sand. The great eagle is long extinct and there hasn't been a sea lion on this beach for years. But still Dyptoe runs.

He hears Marina call from high on the cliff where the ancestral track zig-zags upwards through the flax bushes. Excited, he's about to return her call when he stops. There's a danger he doesn't understand! With his keen yellow eyes he's seen a whirlwind movement at the far end of the beach.

A chill of fear passes from his head to his tail. His head and neck feathers stiffen and rise. Dyptoe races back to the sea!

A dog frolics along the beach, barking, baring teeth and tongue, rolling brown eyes at the wind, at gulls, at a plastic bag that whisks over the sand, even pounding in circles after his own tail.

As Dyptoe disappears to safety under the waves, the dog spots another penguin crossing the beach and the chase is on. The dog snaps, seizing the penguin by the flipper, shaking his prey. As the dog changes grip, somehow the penguin manages to slip away and runs for the sea with the dog in pursuit.

The dog stops and barks at the waves.

Although the penguin has escaped to the sea, he's not safe. A badly ripped flipper means he can't swim, so he can't hunt and he will starve to death.

Cold, dark night falls on the Otago farmland. Sheep baa, rabbits nibble the short grass, lights flash on in the farmhouses and a wooden gate creaks. A dog barks in the distance. Down near the flax bushes creeps a wild tabby cat, hungry for prey. Wind clatters the flax leaves where Marina waits for Dyptoe.

The black-backed gull screeches, the shag wings homeward above the waves. Far out at sea where the albatross glides on the wind, swims Dyptoe.

He swims all night and returns to the land at dawn.

It is late in the winter. Each day Marina and Dyptoe hunt alone at sea and each night they return to land. Sometimes Dyptoe is first back. He preens himself on the rocks and waits for Marina. Sometimes Marina returns first.

Another male penguin is watching her. As she stands on the rocks, he trots past her with his bill low to the ground, his flippers pointing forwards. He stops and stands tall, stretching his neck proudly towards the sky. Then he sneaks a look back over his shoulder to see if he has impressed her.

But Marina ignores him and preens her chest feathers. She waits for Dyptoe.

When she spots Dyptoe leaving the sea, she leans forward and cries loudly to him. He stops at once, answers with all his breath and scampers to the rocks where Marina waits.

They lean towards each other, warbles of welcome deep in their throats. With bills open wide they trumpet louder than the crashing waves, shouting to the sky that they are bonded penguins, the closest of mates. Then they settle to gently preen each other on the cheek, the breast, the head, stopping occasionally to break into joyful trills.

The two penguins stand together facing the sea. They are well-fed, glossy, and as content as penguins can be. The fading winter sun lights up their yellow crowns and sparkles down their shiny blue backs.

Together they waddle along the ancient penguin track. Marina leads. Dyptoe hurries up close behind her, snuggles his head into the back of her neck and flaps his flippers, enclosing her in a penguin hug.

Some distance away, the cries of other penguins peal from the flax bushes. Marina and Dyptoe can hear them but can't see them, for they have tucked themselves away in a special place where it's dark and cool and private.

And this is the way they pass each short day and each long night throughout the Otago winter.

One August day, Marina doesn't go to sea. Instead, she stands near the special place, preening and dozing.

Dyptoe returns by midday. Something mysterious is stirring deep inside him. He collects twigs, grasses and leaves and carries them in his bill to where Marina stands. Behind her, three stout flax bushes grow beside a large rock and it's here that Dyptoe lays his collection.

Wide-eyed, Marina picks up the pieces in her bill and drops them again. For the rest of the afternoon, she shifts them and sorts them.

After a few days, Dyptoe has built a circle with his collection, hollow in the centre, raised at the sides. Marina builds the back wall but Dyptoe rebuilds it to suit himself. As soon as he goes to sea, Marina changes it back again.

One day she settles in the hollow centre of the nest on her belly and flattens herself into the ground. She pokes about the edges with her bill, shifting the pieces yet again and thatching them loosely.

When Dyptoe returns, his greetings are loud and excited. She steps from the nest to preen him. Their necks entwine and with her bill Marina caresses Dyptoe's cheek. Then they break away and shake and trumpet.

Next day, Marina leaves and feeds well at sea. When she returns, she finds Dyptoe filling the nest . . . and he won't move out.

In the morning Dyptoe goes to sea, and while he's gone Marina shifts the entire nest, piece by piece, closer to the rock. She works all day and is resting when Dyptoe returns.

One afternoon while Marina lies in the nest, her eyes peacefully opening and closing, a storm blows in from the sea. The wind rises. Heavy, dark clouds explode into cold August rain.

Dyptoe surfs ashore through crashing breakers and flying foam and runs all the way from the grey sea up the penguin track to Marina.

All night there's rain and storm and the wind-wild dance of the flax bushes. Sections of cliff crack, lift away and slide towards the beach.

At dawn, Marina and some neighbouring penguins head for the sea. But mounds of fallen cliff block the ancient penguin tracks. Penguins call from strange places on the cliff-face trying to get down to the beach. Marina finds a way eventually, but another penguin is so confused by the changes that she can't find her nest. After pacing the beach she heads south and never returns to her mate or the nesting area.

However, Marina and Dyptoe are still together. Their nest is ready and so are they.

Marina stays on land for two days. She lies in the shady nest, head turning slowly, ever watching with her sun-filled eyes. Today, a dapple of spring sunlight dances on her yellow crown feathers. She's as patient as the turquoise ocean that breaks forever on the shore. Just Marina and the sea.

When Dyptoe returns late in the afternoon, she greets him but remains where she is. Dyptoe thrusts his head underneath her, forcing her to stand. In the nest lies one new, pale green egg. He tries to step into the nest but Marina won't budge.

Next morning, he tries again. Finally, Marina steps out and Dyptoe steps in. He stands looking down at the egg between his feet. Marina wanders off along the track for a day at sea.

When she returns, she wants her nest back. Dyptoe won't move over, so she pecks him soundly on the base of the tail. He scrambles out! Marina settles gently over the egg.

Three days later, Marina lays her second egg. The first egg has changed from pale green to dull white.

Now Marina and Dyptoe work together as true partners. One goes to sea while one keeps the eggs warm. Each night they rest together, one on the nest, one close beside. At each changeover they greet and preen and trumpet. As the weeks pass, the warm eggs become dirty and mud-splattered.

On the forty-third day of incubation, when Dyptoe's on the nest and the sun is overhead, a star-shaped fracture appears on one egg. By evening the first fragments of shell break away. Just inside the gap there's a little beak and there are soft squeaking sounds. Marina takes over the nest and looks underneath her whenever there's a squeak. Cracks spread over the shell, and the following evening the shell breaks open.

The first chick lies limp, wet and weak amongst the heap of broken pieces. Marina settles gently over the new baby penguin.

By morning the chick is dry and fluffy dark grey. The webbed feet are palest pink, the eyes are closed and the tiny pink flippers are almost bare. On the tip of the bill there's a white lump, the egg tooth, which the chick used to hammer its way out of the shell.

By evening the second chick has hatched and is drying beneath Marina's warm feathers.

It is early summer. A distance from where Marina and Dyptoe have their nest, two other pairs of penguins have chicks also, just one week old. They watch the world through bright, new eyes. There is darkness, there is warmth, and there is food.

One night a ferret creeps near, attracted by the squeaks of chicks and the smell of fish. She sniffs about with her pointed snout. Her coat is softest fur and her eyes are beady-bright. Handsome is the ferret, but her claws sparkle with sharpness and her white teeth glint back at the cool moon.

She creeps silently along the penguin track and arrives at the first nest. The parent bird lies with his back towards the ferret, settled for the night over the chicks who have just been fed. Nearby the female penguin preens.

The ferret creeps closer. She sees a tiny foot poking out from under the warm feathers of the parent. She pounces, clamps her teeth around the foot and tugs. She drags the chick into the cold and sinks her fangs into the back of its skull. A brief struggle and then nothing more. The parent bird doesn't even notice.

Around the other side, the ferret spots a tiny head peeping out. Again she strikes. She pulls and death-bites the chick, teeth sinking through the down into flesh, into bone. There's warm blood on her whiskered face, her nose, her fur.

17

The ferret drags the bodies away one by one to somewhere dark and secret. Then she heads for the second nest.

This time the penguin who guards his nest turns in time to see the ferret. But his ancestors never knew ferrets and neither does he. He stares at the bushy-tailed movement as the ferret darts in, drags out and kills. She returns for the second chick.

In the ferret's secret place, four dark grey, fluffy baby penguins lie broken, with punctured skulls and sticky, bleeding flesh.

Marina and Dyptoe's nest is some distance away and they know nothing of the ferret's attacks. Their chicks are safe and growing daily.

Each summer's day, one parent hunts at sea and the other guards the chicks.

Today it's Marina who returns well-fed. She calls from the beach. Dyptoe answers from high on the cliff at the nest by the rock. Heavy with food, Marina climbs the steep track, gasping. She stops to hold out her flippers and gaze down at her bright pink feet. She's hot and weary and her chicks need food.

Dyptoe bursts into peals of excited greeting. She answers, but there's no time to preen each other.

The chicks, now four weeks old, stagger towards Marina, squealing for food. Tipodee is always first. He jabs his bill all around Marina's cheeks until Marina opens wide.

Tipodee's bill disappears inside Marina's throat for a few seconds while Marina regurgitates a fishy liquid, salty-sweet. Tipodee takes food three times before his fluffy, grey belly is so swollen that he can hardly move. Immediately Underbelle rushes in and demands her share. Marina gives all that she has.

At last the two chicks stand with heads sunk into shoulders, swaying slightly, their bellies bulging, and cheeks and chests sticky with the fishy food. They'll be satisfied until tomorrow.

By mid-summer, Tipodee and Underbelle are seven weeks old. Now they have stiff, stubby tails and feathers growing beneath the down on their backs and legs. Grey baby fluff lifts off their bodies and is twirled around by the sea breeze.

Each day after feeding, they plead for more, so now it's time for both Marina and Dyptoe to hunt at sea every day. The chicks are left alone.

While their parents are away, the chicks explore the penguin tracks and peep through the flax leaves at the sparkling sea. But when the midday sun blazes upon the dry earth, the chicks stand and gasp in the heat. They can hardly breathe and there's little shade.

Sometimes Marina and Dyptoe reach the shore at the same time, but mostly they arrive alone. When they call, it's the chicks who answer. When they waddle up the penguin path, the hungry chicks rush from the bushes, pleading for food. They peck at each other in a frantic race to reach the parent first.

Once, only once, does Underbelle get the first feed. Tipodee aims a blow at Underbelle with his right flipper. But he misses and somersaults, landing on his back. By the time he's wriggled to his feet, Underbelle is feeding from Dyptoe.

If it has been a bad day for fishing, there is not enough food. The chicks pester their parents long into the night, unsatisfied.

Marina and Dyptoe grow thin and exhausted.

One evening, Dyptoe returns first and feeds the chicks. As usual, Tipodee rushes in and Underbelle has to wait. Dyptoe pulls away from Tipodee to feed Underbelle. When he has no more to offer, he preens himself.

It's nearly night time. Marina is late. Dyptoe calls for her, but only the breakers reply, with roaring and hissing. Underbelle and Tipodee plead for more food. Dyptoe waits, dozes, wakes again, still calls for Marina.

A sea mist puffs into shore and the sea fades away behind it. It is night time. Marina has not yet returned.

Marina has had a wonderful day at sea. She was there when fifteen squid pulsed past. She was there when the school of opal fish flashed in a galaxy of silver spears. She flew through gardens of amber seaweed, through deep sea forests, through caves and canyons and soared back up to the light. She saw dolphins playing and even heard the song of the right whale. After nearly two hundred dives, she's heavy with food and ready to return to land.

A silverside flicks past her and straight ahead. One last catch for Marina.

She surges after it, smooth, streamlined through the water. But suddenly something stops her. She's caught! Pulled to a complete halt! There's a band around her neck. She doesn't understand.

Marina panics! She swirls, pumping her flippers, twirling in circles over and over, spinning, struggling in a fluster of bubbles, while the band around her throat tightens — tightens with each turn.

Marina needs air. Her time underwater is running out. She turns towards the light. But she can't rise.

Gasping, spinning, spiralling, Marina feels the bands close around her throat, her bill, her chest and her yellow crown.

Then the darkness comes over her eyes.

On the surface of the sea, there's a fishing boat. The winch grinds, the drum turns, the net rises. A fisherman untangles the creatures of the sea: seven large gummy sharks, one small octopus, a sea sponge, eighteen red cod, one trumpeter, three squid still squirming, two blue moki, four paddle crabs, one spiny dogfish, a bunch of seaweed — and the body of one yellow-eyed penguin.

All next morning, Dyptoe stays ashore. He waddles slowly down to the waves as if to swim away, but instead he wanders back up the ancestral track. The chicks rush at him, pestering for food, but he turns away.

He leaves the nesting area and finds a place down by the preening rocks where he stands alone, facing the sea. He calls for Marina. But there's only the turquoise ocean sliding in and slipping away forever. Just Dyptoe and the sea.

He wanders along the beach. Then back up the penguin track he climbs and the chicks rush out from the flax bushes.

At last, by mid-afternoon, he enters the waves and by evening he's back. Tipodee is waiting on the penguin track, nearly at the beach. He sees Dyptoe and runs, head bobbing, eyes staring, desperate for food. Dyptoe's nearly pushed off his feet.

Underbelle arrives and presses close, but Tipodee gobbles the stream of food. Dyptoe struggles to pull away and turns towards Underbelle who pecks at his cheeks. Dyptoe feeds her, but there isn't enough.

That night the stars and moon are cloaked by cloud and it is very dark.

Now Dyptoe hunts at sea in the mornings. He passes the afternoons on the preening rocks.

Each day Tipodee reaches Dyptoe first and feeds well. Each day Underbelle grows thinner and weaker, less able to run towards Dyptoe.

On the sixth day, when Tipodee stands aside with bulging belly, Underbelle waddles close to Dyptoe and weakly pecks around his bill. There's a little more food. Out it flows. But because Underbelle is frail, she can't hold her head up to receive the meal and the precious food misses her throat and spills down her feathered chest.

Next day, Underbelle is too weak even to walk. She lies on the earth, a couple of flax bushes away, making soft pleading sounds deep in her throat, while Dyptoe feeds Tipodee.

On the eighth day, the starving chick lies on her belly in the summer heat, moving neither head nor flipper, her bill nudged into the dry earth. She pants. Blowflies buzz about her chest where the spilt food is now caked hard.

In the afternoon, when the heat is fierce, blowflies settle on the chick's head and dabble in the glazed, pale slit of an eye that stares back at the sun.

The summer days pass and Dyptoe continues to feed Tipodee. Some evenings, on his return, Dyptoe lingers on the preening rocks longer than penguins usually do, just watching the sea. Tipodee often meets him there, for now he wanders far from the nesting place. He too stands and just watches the sea.

He has storm-blue feathers over his back and a cloud-white chest. Grey down still fluffs around his neck and over his head. His slate-grey eyes are tinged with pale moonlight.

Sometimes another juvenile penguin joins Tipodee on the rocks. They try out some calls or they rush at each other, bills ready, pretending to peck. Once or twice they've preened each other's cheeks. But they don't concentrate for long before they're off again on their own.

Each day more grey down lifts off Tipodee's head and scuffs over the sand. He now looks much like Dyptoe, but another year must pass before he develops his bright yellow crown. As the summer days grow shorter he sleeps down near the sea. He is four months old.

One morning, after Dyptoe has left and Tipodee is totally alone, he paddles in the sea and stands there looking at the wave-fingers curling around his feet. He lies down like he does on the dusty land. He moves his flippers to steady himself as a wave washes over him, then he surges forward.

The water's deeper now. He can't touch the sand with his chest or feet, so he uses his flippers again, and he's away!

He can swim! He surges streamlined through the breakers and out to the unbroken water. Quite naturally, Tipodee takes breath and dives.

For the next two days he just swims. He dives and rises, floats and plays. On the third day, on a deep dive, he strikes at a flash of silver and Tipodee finds himself with a bill full of food. He's caught his first fish!

Tipodee does not return to the shore. He heads north to explore his new world, fast learning to be a strong swimmer and an able hunter. He won't be ready to breed until he's four or five years old.

When Dyptoe finds Tipodee gone, he settles to preen his feathers. The night is unusually peaceful.

Now Dyptoe does not have to share his meal with any other penguin. He gains a little weight but he moves more slowly. He rests in many places as he climbs the ancestral penguin track. His hunting trips grow shorter and more time is spent on the land. Dyptoe's feathers become ragged, he has no energy and his once golden crown has faded to the colour of sun-bleached sand.

One day, Dyptoe stands in the old nest-bowl by the rock and doesn't go to sea at all. The mornings and evenings are cooler now for the autumn is here.

He stays all night and all the next day, head sunk into shoulders, eyes closed.

Dyptoe hardly moves at all in the shade by the rock. He stands through the passing of the dawn, the crisp morning, the midday sun, the afternoon breezes. He stands like a driftwood statue in the rain and the wind. He stands in the dusk and all through the cool, black night, watching with sunken eyes.

As the days pass, dusty feathers stick out all over his body and his skin is swollen and tender. At the end of the first week, he turns around in the old nest bowl and bruises his flipper on the rock. He bleeds and the blowflies arrive.

By the end of the second week, many feathers have loosened or fallen out to lie all around him like a scattering of snowflakes. He's bedraggled and patchy. He looks like a very old chick, feels like a very sick penguin.

Shadow-thin, Dyptoe is a weary bird, without a mate.

29

But at last his back is covered with neat new rows of shiny blue feathers, for he is moulting.

Dyptoe stirs and flaps his flippers. He stretches his neck and begins to preen his chest. A white silken chest, clean and bright as sea foam.

At the end of the third week, Dyptoe steps from the nest-bowl, now heaped with the debris of the old bird. He walks slowly along the penguin path.

He's a new bird, fresh-born as morning. His back is kingfisher-bright, his swollen flesh is healed and his wonderful penguin crown shimmers golden-yellow in the morning sun.

Patiently, Dyptoe wanders down to the sea. He stands on the rocks, and in his penguin heart, in his penguin way, he's glad just to be there. Glad just to be.

Wind dances on the sea. The bull kelp swings with the wave and lifts like seal flippers, gleams in the sun, rolls like seal heads turning to shore, to sea, then flattens again.

Soon it will be winter. And somewhere out at sea there may be a female penguin looking for a mate.

Dyptoe the yellow-eyed penguin dives. He flies through the yellow water, the green water, the blue water, diving deep down to the inky black water.

When his belly is full, he breathes and dives once more, somersaults in the green water, shoots skywards into the air and arcs down again — all for the joy of it.

This is the way of the yellow-eyed penguin.

31

THE YELLOW-EYED PENGUIN YEAR

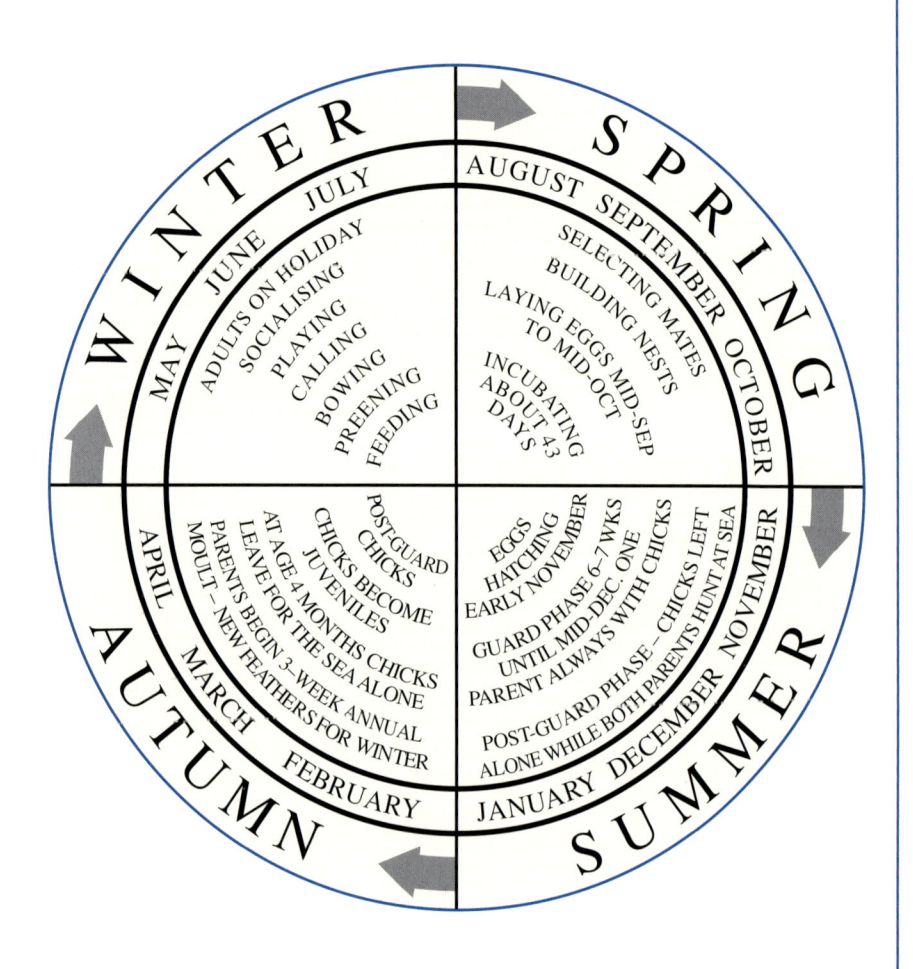

Dedicated to the many people who work to save yellow-eyed penguins

The author wishes to thank Creative New Zealand. Thanks also to Bruce McKinley, Lyn Dowsett, Jim Caldwell, Janice Jones. Special thanks to John Darby and Kerri-Anne Edge.

The yellow-eyed penguin, hoiho (Megadyptes antipodes), stands 55-65cm tall and weighs about 5kg. Females breed at 2-3 years of age and males at 3-5 years. They can live up to 20 years.

Unlike most other penguins, the hoiho does not breed in noisy colonies, but chooses a secluded spot in the forest away from other birds.

Once abundant on the south-east coast of the South Island of New Zealand, the birds are now rare. Their decline is largely due to the loss of their forest habitats and to predators. The estimated population in the South Island is fewer than 650 pairs. The hoiho also lives on Stewart Island and on some Sub-Antarctic islands.

First published by Scholastic New Zealand Limited, 1997
Private Bag 94407, Greenmount, Auckland 1730, New Zealand.

Scholastic Australia Pty Limited
PO Box 579, Gosford, NSW 2250, Australia.

Scholastic Inc
555 Broadway, New York, NY 10012-3999, USA.

Scholastic Canada Ltd
123 Newkirk Road, Richmond Hill, Ontario L4C 3G5, Canada.

Scholastic Limited
1-19 New Oxford Street, London, WC1A 1NU, England.

© Mary Taylor, 1997
ISBN 1-86943-362-9

All rights reserved. No part of this publication may be reproduced or transmitted in any form or by any means, electronic or mechanical, including photocopying, recording, storage in any information retrieval system, or otherwise, without the prior written permission of the publisher.

9 8 7 6 5 4 3 2 1   7 8 9/9 0 1 2 3/0

Edited by Penny Scown.
Typeset in 14/20 Times.
Printed in Hong Kong.